LifeChange Books

TimeBandits

Stuart Briscoe

Multnomah Books

TIME BANDITS
published by Multnomah Books
Published in association with the literary agency of Alive Communications, Inc.
7680 Goddard Street, Suite 200, Colorado Springs, CO 80920.

© 2005 by Stuart Briscoe
International Standard Book Number: 978-0-307-56349-1

Cover design by The DesignWorks Group, Inc.

Italics in Scripture are the author's emphasis.
Scripture quotations are from:
The Holy Bible, New International Version © 1973, 1984 by International Bible Society,
used by permission of Zondervan Publishing House

Published in the United States by WaterBrook Multnomah, an imprint of the Crown
Publishing Group, a division of Random House Inc., New York.

MULTNOMAH and its mountain colophon are registered trademarks of Random House Inc.

Printed in the United States of America

For information:
MULTNOMAH BOOKS
12265 Oracle Boulevard, Suite 200
Colorado Springs, CO 80921

Library of Congress Cataloging-in-Publication Data

Briscoe, D. Stuart.
  Time bandits / by Stuart Briscoe.
     p. cm.
  ISBN 978-1-60142-672-7
  1. Time management—Religious aspects—Christianity. 2. Kingdom of God.
I. Title.
  BV4598.5.B75 2005
  640'.43—dc22

                                   2004024357

Dedicated to the memory of my parents,
Stanley and Mary Briscoe, who by example and teaching
instilled in me from my earliest days the absolute
necessity to be focused and committed to clearly
defined priorities if I was to live a full life.
I am grateful to and for them.

Contents

Chapter One

SURROUNDED BY MASKED MEN

"What's your biggest problem?"

The question was as surprising as it was direct. I had just spent more than an hour with a young reporter who, having concluded the interview and packed away his notes, was on his way out the door when he wheeled round and caught me off guard. *My biggest problem?* I thought frantically. "Establishing priorities," I blurted out without thinking.

He nodded and left.

The question lingered for the rest of the day. I was aware that my life was not without problems, and my wife was probably aware of a number that escaped my attention. But the biggest one? What was it? I wished I had been given more time to think before answering. But the more I thought about it, the more convinced I became that my knee-jerk answer was probably correct.

I knew I had problems with priorities!

Each day there were things I knew that I *had* to do—no question. Then there were things I thought I really *ought* to do, plus things that I desperately *wanted* to do. Added to that were the things I imagined other people *expected* me to do and yet more things that others *insisted* I do. And so on! But—and here I consoled myself soulfully—"there aren't enough hours in the day!"

> I had been forced into a situation where the demands of life exceeded the supply of time.

The result, of course, was that many things were left undone, and some were only half done. Sometimes critical things were missed while I attended to things of less significance. I often disappointed others and frustrated myself.

Each morning I woke up feeling like the cowboy who rode up to a saloon, hitched his horse to the rail, started to pull a bag of oats over the horse's head, and heard the town drunk standing nearby say, "Any fool can see you'll never fit that horse in that bag!"

My horse would not fit my bag.

I had been forced into a situation where the demands of life exceeded the supply of time. "That's the problem!" I decided. "If I had more time, I could get everything done." But then I wondered if that was true. Would it not mean that having been given more time I would find—or be presented with—more things to do?

But if more hours in the day would not fix the problem, what would? It seemed to me that the only possibility of an answer lay in the way the hours given to me were being used.

And that's the point when I began to sniff out the banditry under my roof. Time bandits? That had to be it! I (as everyone else on the planet) was granted a set number of hours each day that could be used, abused, invested, or wasted. I knew that. But some days it seemed as if I was held hostage by demands and interruptions, crises and trivialities, diversions and frustrations that surrounded me like masked men ominously demanding my time and robbing me of my day.

Bandits! Thieves! Robbers!

I was the pastor of a growing church at that time, and it seemed that many people were interested in what I did with my life. Rightly so…well, to a point. One day I was approached by a group of very fit looking men who said, "Stuart, we believe your physical fitness is very important, because if your body quits, your ministry ends. Wouldn't you agree?" I did! Promptly! "Good," they replied, "we are all football coaches, and we have worked out an exercise routine for you that we'd like to do with you each morning. Physical fitness is a priority!"

Round about the same time, a well-read lady in the congregation said to me, "Stuart, we understand that the preacher's job is to listen to what God is saying and then relate it to his contemporaries. Now, we think you're very good at listening to what God says in the Bible, but you're not really in tune with American culture. So we have enrolled you in a book club because we believe reading and meditating is a priority. Don't you agree?"

"Oh yes," I replied with conviction and a sinking feeling.

Another kind person told me that he had been reading about Martin Luther, who had apparently said on one occasion that he had so many things to do that day that he could not *possibly* manage on less than—I think it was—three hours of prayer. He then added enthusiastically, "Stuart, you're such an activist, but we wonder if you're spending enough time in prayer. Prayer is such a priority, isn't it?"

"Yes," I replied dutifully, overcome with guilt.

On another occasion the parents of a happy, healthy family said to me, "Stuart, we really appreciate the way you serve us so faithfully, but we suspect that you might be neglecting your own family. Are you spending enough time with them? Remember that if you succeed as a pastor and fail as a father, your testimony will be ruined. You really need to spend more time with your own children. Remember, they are your priority!" I remembered!

And then, would you believe that a dear little lady said to me, "Stuart, you look exhausted. Are you getting enough rest and relaxation? Remember that God worked for six days and then rested the seventh. If you carry on the way you're going, you will burn out in no time. Proper rest is a priority, you know!"

I knew!

But—and it was a big *but*—how could I possibly fit it all in? Maybe I could run with my kids, take along a book and read it as I ran with one eye open, and pray at the same time with the other one shut— oh yes, and all the time resting!

But—and it was a big but—how could I possibly fit it all in?

I was familiar with the well-known "God first, family second, work third" formula, but I found that while it was fundamentally sound, it did not always work. I knew, for instance, that Vince Lombardi, the legendary coach of the Green Bay Packers, believed in a "trinity of life" that was made up of "God, family, and the Green Bay Packers." According to his biographer, "He placed them in that order." But in reality his family "usually came in third, unable to compete in his heart and mind with his dual passions of God and the Packers."[1] I had also read somewhere about Ray Kroc, the founder of McDonald's. He told a reporter that his priorities were "God first, family second, and McDonald's third," but then he added that when he went into the office, the order was reversed. Apparently these highly successful men had problems with their priorities, too. At least I was in good company. I took some comfort from that, but not much!

When you're surrounded by time bandits, it's good to have company.

1.   David Marannis, *When Pride Still Mattered* (New York: Touchstone Press, 1999), 242–3.

Chapter Two

FIRST THE KINGDOM

My mother was a very organized lady and at times despaired of her disorganized son. She used to say regularly, "First things first!" The problem was, how did I decide when a "thing" was a "first thing"? When I arrived at a conclusion, I often discovered that my mother's opinion did not exactly coincide with mine. Nevertheless, her words—"first things first"—remained embedded in the dim recesses of my subconscious.

I sincerely wanted to operate on that principle, but for many years I was only frustrated by it. I suppose I gave up thinking about it and developed a sort of ad hoc approach to priorities. My life began to resemble the frantic efforts of the man in the circus who starts plates spinning and then rushes from one to another trying desperately to keep everything in motion.

Then one fine day I read something that made a dramatic difference—and still does. It was in the Sermon on the Mount, which, as its name suggests, records one of Jesus' sermons—or possibly a compilation of His sayings. Jesus was talking about His Father's concern for people. I read:

> "Seek first his kingdom and his righteousness, and
> all these things will be given to you as well."
>
> MATTHEW 6:33

"First things first" resurfaced from my memory bank and rested next to Christ's words: "First his kingdom."

First things first—first His kingdom.

There was a certain resonance between the two brief statements. They seemed to fit. I wondered if it was possible that Jesus was really talking about something as relevant to modern-day existence as priorities. Was He actually saying that the "first thing" is the Father's kingdom? And that everything else follows the king-

Was Jesus really talking about something as relevant to modern-day existence as priorities?

dom? That it was not a case of first, second, third? Perhaps the kingdom was what really mattered, and everything else was less important. This was well worth considering carefully. It wasn't that I was learning something new. I'd known this from my parents ever since I had known anything. But as I moved into more responsible years and began to take life a little more seriously, I needed to think more carefully about how I was living it.

I started by reading the verse in its context. I knew enough about reading the Bible to know that you can make it say just about anything you want it to say if you dig up words from their setting and replant them where they don't belong. This is what Jesus said:

> "Therefore I tell you, do not worry about your life, what you will eat or drink; or about your body, what you will wear. Is not life more important than food, and the body more important than clothes? Look at the birds of the air; they do not sow or reap or store away in barns, and yet your heavenly Father feeds them. Are you not much more valuable than they? Who of you by worrying can add a single hour to his life?
>
> "And why do you worry about clothes? See how the lilies of the field grow. They do not labor or spin. Yet I tell you that not even Solomon in all

his splendor was dressed like one of these. If that is how God clothes the grass of the field, which is here today and tomorrow is thrown into the fire, will he not much more clothe you, O you of little faith? So do not worry, saying, 'What shall we eat?' or 'What shall we drink?' or 'What shall we wear?' For the pagans run after these things, and your heavenly Father knows that you need them. *But seek first his kingdom and his righteousness, and all these things will be given to you as well.* Therefore do not worry about tomorrow, for tomorrow will worry about itself. Each day has enough trouble of its own."

MATTHEW 6:25–34

I realized that Jesus was addressing priorities with people because they were in danger of getting them wrong. If the people weren't corrected, they might make the fatal mistake of putting less important things in the most important place and all-important issues among unimportant issues.

So how do we decide what is all-important as opposed to what is less important or unimportant? That's like determining what is straight as opposed to crooked, what is level as opposed to sloping. You need a measure, a standard. And that is exactly what Jesus gave the people: *The kingdom is first, and everything else is second, at best!*

My initial reaction was to think, *Well, that sounds fine, but it's impractical. Jesus seems to be spiritualizing everything and saying that the kingdom is where the real action is and everything else is insignificant, but we still have to live our lives. We can't go around thinking about the kingdom while ignoring the essential practicalities of life.* However, Jesus was not saying that the everyday concerns of life are unimportant and should be ignored. He never asks us to float above reality in a benign cloud of denial while we think about some kind of esoteric kingdom.

On the contrary, He was giving careful attention to "all these things," assuring the people that the heavenly Father was well aware of them and involved in addressing them. If they put the kingdom first, "all these things" would be addressed in their proper time and place. He was not saying that these legitimate issues were unimportant—just *less* important.

As I thought about this remarkably simple but profound principle, I recognized that I had a lot of rethinking, unthinking, and de-thinking to do. First things first—first His kingdom! Hmm…

Chapter Three

WHAT'S FIRST
RIGHT NOW?

Recognizing that you might have gotten things the wrong way around can have a sobering effect. Majoring on minors may mean making major mistakes. Jesus was very clear on this when He pointed out that to worry about what you will wear and not give any thought to where your life is heading is folly (see Matthew 6:25). It's even worse than being "all dressed up with nowhere to go." Even more significantly, Jesus reminded people that to build up treasure on earth and be bankrupt in heaven is disastrous. Why? For lots of reasons. Not least the fact that the treasure you amass on earth you leave there, and the value you accrue in heaven counts for eternity.

In the old days, when bandits held up a stagecoach, they would shout, "Your money or your life!" while holding everyone at gunpoint. A decision of that nature was not too difficult to make! But as I read Jesus' words, I realized that time bandits don't give that option. They want your "money *and* your life"—your time *and* your eternal destiny. They'll take your precious earthly minutes *and* your priceless heavenly reward!

And the place they'll always start is with your priorities.

The smart thing to do first is to evaluate the priorities you already have in place. At least that way you can give yourself a chance to make any midcourse corrections that may be called for, rather like astronauts on their way to the moon. They know that being just a degree off course at the beginning of their journey will mean missing the moon by *a lot* a few days later. So they continually check and make the necessary corrections to keep them on track.

But before we can evaluate our priorities we need to identify them. In His sermon, Jesus was extremely helpful in this regard. Granted, He didn't actually use the word *priority,* but He did show how to identify them. He talked about:

> Time bandits want your "money _and_ your life"—your time _and_ your eternal destiny.

ANXIETIES

Jesus said:

- "Do not *worry* about your life." (Matthew 6:25)
- "Who of you by *worrying* can add a single hour to his life?" (v. 27)
- "Why do you *worry* about clothes?" (v. 28)
- "Do not *worry*, saying, 'What shall we eat? ' or 'What shall we drink?' or 'What shall we wear?'" (v. 31)
- "Do not *worry* about tomorrow." (v. 34)

Now I wonder, why was Jesus stressing *worry*? Presumably because it was a major issue among the people of His day. But they—as well as we—only worried about the things that were important to them. So if you identify an anxiety, you've discovered a priority!

It's most interesting to see the kind of things the people of long ago used to worry about:

- Food—what shall we eat?
- Fashion—what shall we wear?
- Fitness—adding a single hour to life.
- Future—worrying about tomorrow.
- Finances—storing up treasures on earth.

Sound familiar? Of course it does. And it points out the inescapable fact that little has changed over the centuries.

People understandably focus on the essential practicalities of life. They are priorities in most people's lives. But are they as important as we make them?

Bottom line—if it's an anxiety it's a priority.

ACTIVITIES

Jesus also addressed the fact that the birds "do not sow or reap or store away in barns" and the lilies do not "labor and spin," yet both birds and flowers are well cared for. Not that Jesus was disparaging hard work. Neither was He suggesting that we should expect our food to drop out of heaven on a golden platter. But He *was* telling the people that because the birds and the flowers are cared for by their heavenly Father, people should have a keener focus on Him and put less emphasis on the activities that demand so much of their time and energy and accordingly become a priority.

You may react to this and say, "Whoa, hold on a minute. Was Jesus saying that if you spend time working hard to look after your family, you've got your priorities wrong? That you should just trust God to feed, clothe, and house them? And pay for their college tuition?!" No, of course not. But He was saying that a life bound up in mundane practicalities at the expense of loftier issues is a life based on misplaced priorities.

For our purposes, let's accept the fact that activities can be a measure of priorities. For example, leaving aside legitimate necessary activities, I think most people agree that we all have varying amounts of discretionary time—the time left over when we can do what we *want* rather than what we *must*. The activities we engage in during discretionary time certainly tell us a lot about our priorities. As has been said, "We can always find time to do what we really want to do!"

This reminds me of the days when I used to play Rugby. There was an old man who supported our team through thick and thin—and rain, snow, sleet, and hail! He never missed a game, huddled in an overcoat, his face turning red, blue, purple, and puce as the game wore on. His daughter told me that he regularly sang in the church choir on Sunday, the day after the match, and often had a severe cold on Monday. As he lay in bed coughing and spluttering, he would growl, "Those choir stalls in the church are too drafty. I'm quitting the choir!" No mention of the gale blowing across the Rugby ground!

Bottom line—our activities (particularly during discretionary time) identify our priorities.

AMBITIONS

When Jesus said that the pagans "run after" all these things and then immediately, by way of contrast, insisted that we should "seek" first the kingdom, He used the same word— a strong word. It means a lot more than to casually look for and slightly less than to be obsessed by. In other words, He was talking about people being ambitious for or earnestly desirous of certain things—things that matter a lot to them. *Or priorities.*

I have a grandson whose ambition was to make the varsity soccer team as a sophomore. He did it, as a starter and a standout! Then he aimed to be captain as a junior. He's done that too! I know men whose earnest desire/obsession/priority was to be a millionaire by thirty. And they've done it. But in these examples—and a thousand other cases—goals are met and ambitions are achieved when other things are made secondary and the prime objective is clearly defined.

Bottom line—put your finger on an ambition, and you've got hold of a priority.

So anxieties, activities, and ambitions are pointers to existing priorities. We all have them. We need to evaluate them because we wouldn't want to major on minors—and find out too late.

If you want to fight off the time bandits, learn their techniques, check for their fingerprints, and follow them to their hideouts. In other words, *recognize* where your time is going.

It has something to do with your existing priorities—and some of them are hiding behind masks.

Chapter Four

WHAT'S THE KINGDOM?

Two men playing golf were chatting between shots. "How's your wife?" inquired one of them.

"Compared to what?" the other replied.

Not quite politically correct, I realize, but there's a point that is worth noting. When we talk about evaluating priorities because our existing priorities may be misplaced, we need something against which to measure their validity. So the question, "How are your priorities?" may require the answer, "Compared to what?"

In insisting "Seek first his kingdom," Jesus was saying in effect, "Don't worry about life's details while ignoring life's meaning. Don't expend energy that should be spent on matters of lasting significance on things that have no lasting value." But who decides the meaning of life, and who determines whether or not things have lasting value? This is where the kingdom comes into the equation.

The thrust of Jesus' message was that the kingdom is the plumb line, and everything should be compared to it. The kingdom is central, and everything should revolve around it. The kingdom is the standard, and everything should be measured by it. But what did He mean by *the kingdom*? Which one was He referring to? There were many kingdoms in His day. Even His closest followers had problems at this point.

> The kingdom is the standard, and everything should be measured by it.

Let's remind ourselves what Jesus actually said: "Seek first *his* kingdom and *his* righteousness." Whose kingdom? Who is the "He"? The context shows that He was talking about "the heavenly Father" and His "kingdom." Or, if you like, "the kingdom of God" or "the kingdom of heaven."

Some people see the "kingdom of God" (favored by Mark and Luke) and the "kingdom of heaven" (preferred by Matthew) as two separate realities. But there is good reason to believe that the two terms refer to the same reality. Matthew's preference for the "kingdom of heaven" over the "kingdom of God" may be explained by the fact that he was writing primarily for Jewish Christians who traditionally used *heaven* as a synonym for *God,* owing to their reluctance to use the divine name (some theologians call this practice a circumlocution).

So what was Jesus saying? He was saying precisely what He spent a great amount of time saying, namely that the kingdom of God is a reality that must transcend all other realities.

But what exactly did He mean by "the kingdom of God"? The message of the Bible centers around the struggle between the benevolent forces of good and righteousness and the malevolent forces of evil and unrighteousness. And behind these "forces" is the awesome reality of the conflict between God and the devil.

That Jesus believed in the devil is beyond question. He had met the devil in a monumental confrontation in the desert shortly after His baptism and entry into public ministry, and during the years of ministry He made it very clear that the devil and his emissaries were violently opposed to His mission. So when He exorcised demonic forces from a blind mute, He stated unequivocally, "If I drive out demons by the Spirit of God, then the kingdom of God has come upon you" (Matthew 12:28). In other words, He was telling the Pharisees that they had seen a demonstration of power greater than the powers of evil. This greater power was nothing more than the power of God at work in their midst. Before their eyes. They could not refute it.

So "kingdom" and "power" were related in Jesus' mind, and the connection between the two was presented to the onlookers in dramatic fashion. The kingdom of God was all about the power of God being demonstrated in the middle of the territory that the devil had been claiming as his own. The place where men and women and boys and girls lived out their everyday lives. Jesus had come to counter the devil's activity and restore the control and the power and the rule of God where formerly the devil had reigned supreme.

Jesus knew that the struggle would be long and fierce, but He also recognized that ultimately God would win and His kingdom would be established. With this in mind, He taught His disciples to keep their focus on God's ultimate victory by praying, "Your kingdom come, your will be done on earth as it is in heaven" (Matthew 6:10).

No one should have been surprised by this, because John the Baptist, the forerunner of Jesus, had warned the people that the kingdom was about to break into their lives, and Jesus himself started His preaching ministry by forcefully proclaiming the same thing. Right from the beginning He had preached, "The kingdom of God is near."

But you might be asking, "What on earth does this

have to do with me and my priorities?" I'm glad you asked.

During the Gulf War in 1991 and the subsequent Iraq War in 2003, much of the fighting by the coalition troops was done from thirty thousand feet or more, from a distance where the pilots could not even see their targets. Even more amazing, the central command post for these operations was in Florida, thousands of miles away! But it became apparent that the war could not be carried out solely from such long range. As the military people put it, they needed "boots on the ground." So the infantry, the paratroopers, and the marines moved in.

Now the war fought by the commanders in Florida and by the "boots on the ground" was the same war. But to the Florida brass and the ground forces, the war meant something *very* different. Like the difference between going home for lunch and being away from home for a year. Like the difference between being frustrated by a capricious computer and having your head shot off.

In a similar way, the struggle between God and the devil or even between good and evil is being waged at one level, but you and I are the "boots on the ground." We are in the line of fire.

And what does that mean? Simply put, it means that we may be more vulnerable to malevolent forces than we realize and therefore more in need of divine intervention than we may have grasped.

And we are not only thinking of the meddling of demons and other spiritual forces. Our own misplaced priorities and warped thinking and clouded perceptions are at times our worst enemies. Whatever and whoever subverts us living our lives under the control and power of the living God is truly a time bandit!

How can these foes be countered? By the recognition that the kingdom of God—that is, His power and rule, His counteracting might, and His truth-induced restructuring and reordering of our lives—is imperative. Or perhaps we should say, "Recognizing the kingdom of God as a personal reality is the first thing that must be put first."

We often have a tendency to think of such things as the kingdom of God in an abstract sense rather than embracing its powerful reality. We're rather like the man who after laying a fresh concrete driveway showered and was relaxing reading the paper when he noticed a small boy carefully walking through the soft concrete. He rushed outside and filled the air with less than complimentary comments about the young man and his activities. The vicar happened to be walking past and said rather superciliously, "I thought you loved young people."

"I do," replied the irate gentleman, "but in the abstract—not in my concrete!"

Chapter Five

SEEKING THE KINGDOM

The battle was fierce and bloody at Bosworth on 22 August 1485. The forces of Henry Tudor, Earl of Richmond, had engaged the much larger army of King Richard III of England and had prevailed. Many of Richard's soldiers, sickened by his deceit, treachery, and murder, had deserted him. He had fought bravely, but in close-quarter combat, his horse had been slain beneath him. Horseless in the midst of battle was no place for a king to be. Seeking to make himself heard in the din of war, he shouted above the fray, "A horse! A horse! My kingdom for a horse!" (At least, in Shakespeare's dramatic version this is what he said.)

Gaining the kingdom had been Richard's inglorious

obsession. He had schemed, betrayed, and deceived. He had committed murder—some said he murdered his own wife. He was probably guilty of infanticide—he was widely suspected of being responsible for the deaths of the young princes in the Tower. He had hacked and hewn his way to the throne. And his hands were indelibly stained with the blood of countless innocent victims.

But now his pursuit of a kingdom glorifying himself was rapidly arriving at a terminus. And suddenly the kingdom was negotiable. At that moment he needed a fiery charger. Failing that, any old hack would do. If anybody would give him a horse so that he could save his own skin, they could have the kingdom. For what good is a kingdom to a corpse? In fact, the kingdom was more than negotiable; it was expendable. The possession of a kingdom that had dominated his adult life and driven him to unspeakable excesses was now of no consequence. A horse was all he wanted. To get away and save his skin. He had sought a kingdom and won a kingdom, but now it was utterly valueless.

By way of contrast, let me remind you of a couple of stories told by that master storyteller—Jesus. In Jesus' day, before radio, television, newspapers, or paperbacks, a good storyteller was a huge attraction. He not only filled many a long hour in the dark evenings, but he passed on traditions and functioned as teacher and moral guide. Jesus was a master storyteller and delighted in telling parables, which enlightened the concerned and did little more than entertain the curious. In my school days, we were taught that a parable is an earthly story with a heavenly meaning. One of my classmates who was not paying attention when asked to define a parable said, "I think it's a heavy story with an earthy meaning." Not quite!

Anyway, Jesus told lots of parables. And many of His stories—or parables—started with the same formula, "The kingdom of heaven is like…" Some were quite lengthy and detailed and others remarkably brief and to the point. The two I have in mind are short and unambiguously pointed!

> "The kingdom of heaven is like treasure hidden in a field. When a man found it, he hid it again, and then in his joy went and sold all he had and bought that field. Again, the kingdom of heaven is like a merchant looking for fine pearls. When he found one of great value, he went away and sold everything he had and bought it."
>
> MATTHEW 13:44–46

Stranded without a horse in the middle of a battle, the kingdom of England was worth no more than a horse. But to the two men in Jesus' stories, the kingdom of heaven—or the kingdom of God—was worth *everything*.

The value we place on something will determine the

degree of passion we show for that thing. Something of limited value is readily made negotiable, and once that happens, it becomes quickly expendable under the right circumstances. On the other hand, something of infinite worth is deeply desired and tenaciously held on to through thick and thin.

By telling these two stories, Jesus made it clear that He expects people to see the possession of the kingdom as of such worth that it becomes all-important to them. And they pursue it with a passion.

> Jesus expects people to see the possession of the kingdom as all-important.

That leads to the obvious question—what is it about the kingdom that makes it so valuable that people pursue it with a passion? There are many answers to that question, but let me tell you about something the apostle Paul wrote in a letter to the church in Colossae. He told the people there that they should be "joyfully giving thanks to the Father" because He has "qualified you to share in the inheritance of the saints in the kingdom of light. For he has rescued us from the dominion of darkness and brought us into the kingdom of the Son he loves, in whom we have redemption, the forgiveness of sins" (Colossians 1:11–14).

Without going into a lot of detail, we can easily see a number of immensely valuable things that God does for people:

- *He qualifies them* to share in the inheritance of the saints. Saints are not necessarily the rather anemic looking gentlemen in stained glass windows, but ordinary people who, having committed themselves to the grace of God, have been set apart by Him for His purposes. Accordingly they have a sense of divine calling on their lives, and their inheritance guarantees that they have all they need to fulfill it. So they are enriched with a sense of purpose and direction, adequacy and confidence.

- *He rescues them* from the dominion of darkness. You've probably heard people say when they don't understand something or they have not been informed about it, "I'm completely in the dark about that." There is a sense in which people created by God can live their lives so estranged from Him they are completely in the dark about many things. This darkness becomes a "dominion," or a dominating factor, in that being in the dark about the God who created them, they are in the dark about *why* they were created and as a result their lives lack coherence, significance, and purpose. But to be delivered into the "kingdom of light" not only introduces people to the knowledge of God, but also ushers them into a recognition of who they are and why they are who they are. You could say, "They've seen the light!"

- *He brings them* into the kingdom of the Son He loves. Imagine being introduced to an environment permeated by divine love. That's the environment of the kingdom. And how is that love demonstrated to those who are brought into the kingdom? By redemption and the forgiveness of sins. When a professional athlete makes a serious mistake, he becomes the "goat." But should he then produce a spectacular play, he morphs immediately into a "hero," and we are usually told he has redeemed himself. We can't redeem ourselves in the eyes of God because our sins can only be forgiven *by God*. But He is willing to do that for kingdom people and redeem them. So they are no longer "goats," but become "the sheep of His pasture," warmly and wonderfully cared for by the Good Shepherd.

Put all that together and you begin to get some little idea of the enormous value of the kingdom and the quality of experience offered to kingdom people. It's all about your past being forgiven, your destiny being secured, and your life in the interim being filled with purpose and direction, adequacy and blessing, and lived out in the warmth of the Father's love. Such value, such worth generates a desire for such riches, a seeking after or a passion for the kingdom. And that becomes the top priority.

Did I say "priority"?

Remember, this is where the bandits sneak in the door! And if we're not careful, if we're not vigilant, those wretched thieves will not only rob us of our time; they will blindfold us so we cannot see the blessings of the kingdom. They will handcuff us with small ambitions and easily lead us uncomplaining and unawares, captive to a life less than full of the blessing God has in mind for us.

Don't let them get away with it!

Don't stand idly by while a gang of thieves steals the joy and beauty, wealth and wonder, right out of your Christian life. When we see what these bandits are doing and where our priorities are taking us, we must be smart enough to take drastic measures—and there's no time to lose.

We must take steps to channel our interests, our passion, and our desires into paths of importance and ways of blessing. We should seek the kingdom—with a passion.

And when we do, we have the bandits on the run.

Chapter Six

WHERE TO START?

A rather nervous speaker invited to address a group of students began his speech apologetically, "I'm afraid I have so many things to say to you today that I don't know where to begin."

"Then start near the end," one of the students suggested helpfully.

Now, there is no doubt that if time were of the utmost importance, starting near the end was an admirable suggestion. But if a desire to get the message were a primary concern, then starting near the beginning would obviously be more beneficial.

So let's assume out of a concern for a balanced life based on sound priorities, which requires an understanding of what it means to put the kingdom first, that we really *want* to know where to begin.

Let's begin one dark night a couple thousand years ago. Jesus is relaxing after a busy day among the people. They have been anxious to hear what He has to say and even more anxious to find solutions to their personal problems. But this is draining work, and He needs time and space to replenish.

Quietly and almost furtively, a distinguished elderly gentleman seeks Jesus out in His quiet place. Addressing the carpenter of Nazareth as "Rabbi," he introduces himself. The gentleman in question is none other than Nicodemus, the highly regarded "teacher of Israel." To be called "Rabbi" by such a man is no mean compliment, and it is obvious that the older man's desire to speak to the much younger man stems from genuine concern. He adds further compliments to his opening address by identifying the work that Jesus is doing as evidence of God being with Him. In doing this, he demonstrates the greatest respect for the young preacher.

Amazingly Jesus brusquely responds, "No one can see the kingdom of God unless he is born again" (John 3:3). This is strong meat, and Nicodemus is taken aback. Who wouldn't be?

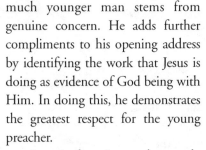

Being "born again" is the way you "see" and "enter" the kingdom.

able. Perhaps the best way for religious people who struggle with the concept to look at the issue is to recognize that Nicodemus himself was a deeply devoted religious man of the highest repute, but according to Jesus he needed to be born again.

Of course some of the objections of religious people stem from what they see as religious excess on the part of some "born again" advocates. They have been given—or have at least gained—the impression that being born again is all about a dramatic, life-changing, emotionally charged event. Let's face it, for some people it is. And it needs to be! But for many it is a quiet process over a period of time as the soul is made aware of spiritual need, as the mind is enlightened to spiritual truth, as the emotions are nerved to deep-rooted longing, and as the will is molded into glad submission to the King establishing His kingdom.

Then there are the people—and they are numerous—who have diminished and degraded the wonderful truth of regeneration. It started when Jimmy Carter ran for president. He was very straightforward about the fact that he had been "born again." Many people had no idea what he was talking about, so they resorted to ridicule, which is one of the first defenses of the ignorant. A born again reporter covering Carter's run for the White House, however, knew what was going on, wrote up a glossary of terms that Carter was using and made them available.

In no time everybody was talking authoritatively on the subject. Or so they thought. But very soon to be born again meant nothing more than to have a new start. So an athlete recovered from a broken leg on returning to the team was a "born again" wide receiver, an alcoholic on leaving the Betty Ford Center a "born again" alcoholic, and a businessman coming out of Chapter 11 bankruptcy was a "born again" businessman.

But being born again is infinitely more than making a new start or turning over a new leaf. It's all about yielding to God's grace, receiving His forgiveness, and welcoming His Spirit into the inner recesses of life—there to rule and reign and produce a life lived in dependence rather than independence.

If the kingdom must be first—if we're to stop those time bandits—then the very first part of the kingdom being first must be ensuring that we are born again.

Chapter Seven

WHAT NOW?

I was born on November 9 in the year of our Lord 1930 in a small town called Millom, which is perched precariously between the mountains and the Irish Sea on the southernmost tip of Cumberland, the most northern county of England. As was not unusual for women in those far off days, my mother was delivered of her firstborn—me—by a midwife in the front bedroom of our home above the grocery store where my parents earned their bread and butter. This room, as I remember, seemed to be reserved exclusively for such auspicious events. And as I was the firstborn, the furniture was as new.

November 9, 1930, also happened to be Armistice Day, the day when parades and speeches and floral tributes expressed the appreciation of the living for those who gave their lives in World War I. I am told—my memory is hazy on this point—that at the moment of my entry into the world the local town band was marching past our home blowing lustily on their battered instruments. Not exactly celebrating my arrival, but at least giving me a rousing welcome.

Why do I bring this up? Mainly to make a point. And the point is? My recollections of my birth are based entirely on hearsay. And yet I am adamantly convinced that I was born. Not simply because those who told me the details were very reliable people. More than that. I am sure that I was born because I am alive! Or to put it another way—the indisputable evidence of birth is life.

Now, here's the point. If an analogy can be drawn between being born and being born again, another analogy can be assumed. The second analogy is that if the evidence of birth is life, the evidence for being born again is living anew.

Some of the people who object to "born again" teaching complain that some of the proponents of this so called life-changing experience show little or no evidence of having been changed. The two infamous Jims—Jimmy Swaggart and Jim Bakker—are regularly produced as exhibits 1 and 2. and the critics, of course, have a point. And this point is not always adequately stressed. Being born again is not just about an experience—of varying degrees of intensity. It is about a change of direction and orientation that leads to a gradually but discernibly transformed life. Now if the kingdom is the top priority, it follows that experiencing new birth is where it starts, and demonstrating a new life is where it continues. This then becomes the ongoing top priority.

But the critics who want to see more than they are being shown at times also need to remember that newborn babies spend a while just lying there before they sit up, spend more time surveying the scene before they stand up, and even longer before they are ready to run a marathon. Born-again people must be allowed time to develop the new life. And this is not to excuse failure; it is to allow realistically for growth and maturity.

> It is not just the kingdom of God that is a priority, but also the "righteousness" of God.

What did Jesus say on this issue? Let's go back to the key verse:

> "Seek first his kingdom and his righteousness, and all these things will be given to you as well."
>
> MATTHEW 6:33

Immediately we see that it is not just the kingdom of God that is a priority, but also the "righteousness" of God. What does this mean? The expression "the righteousness of

God" can mean the "rightness" of God's being and character and therefore His actions. But it can also mean the gift God gives the repentant unrighteous person who trusts Christ for salvation. That person is declared "right with God." The third meaning, however, is the one Jesus uses in this verse. Here the righteousness of God is the standard of behavior of those who have received the gift of righteousness and as a result are behaving rightly before God. To the Jewish people, living before God meant living in the community of God's people. So we can add "treating people rightly" to "living rightly before God." So in summary, the righteousness of God can be an attribute of God, a gift of God, or living rightly before God among people.

You may wonder why we should pick the third way of understanding what Jesus said, and the answer is because of the context in which He used the term:

- "Blessed are those who hunger and thirst after *righteousness* for they shall be filled" (Matthew 5:6).
- "Blessed are those who are persecuted because of *righteousness* for theirs is the kingdom of heaven" (5:10).
- "I tell you that unless your *righteousness* surpasses that of the Pharisees and the teachers of the law, you will certainly not enter the kingdom of heaven" (5:20).

- "Be careful not to do your acts of *righteousness* before men to be seen by them" (6:1).

In each of these cases, Jesus was talking about behavior, about lifestyle. We can therefore deduce from His powerful statement that expressing the kingdom in lifestyle should be the natural priority following the initial priority of experiencing the kingdom in the new birth.

When I was eighteen, the Korean War broke out and the British government instituted the draft. Accordingly, I was required to present myself at a military medical center, where I was duly poked and prodded, twisted and turned, and declared A1. I was then asked if I had a preference as to which branch of the military I would like to join. As I had given no thought to such an important topic, I said no and was told, "Then pick one."

It so happened that there was a fine looking man standing there in the uniform of the Royal Marines and—I blush to admit it all these years later—I thought to myself, *I would look good in that uniform.* And that is how I became a Royal Marine!

Well, that's not quite right. Because once I reported to Chatham Barracks, I discovered, first, that they did not have one of those uniforms for me and, second, that they were clearly less than impressed with me as a Royal Marine. Many weeks later, covered with blisters and wracked with backaches, headaches, and heartaches, I was finally declared fit to go outside the barracks wearing the uniform. It had been drilled into me that if I was going to call myself a Marine and wear the uniform of this elite Corps, I had better behave like a Marine. And if I did not do that, I would bring disgrace to the uniform and dishonor to the Corps and no little discomfort to my person. Heavy stuff for an eighteen-year-old. But I learned a powerful lesson in those days long ago.

If you're going to profess, you'd better perform.

And that becomes a priority for a kingdom person.

Chapter Eight

WATCHING YOUR STEP

Let me tell you one of my favorite stories. I'm sure it's apocryphal, but don't let that spoil it.

One day, the king's sons were playing in Hyde Park, London. The elder brother said to his younger royal sibling, "I'll bet you a shilling that all fat policemen have bald heads."

"You're on," replied the prince.

Obligingly a fat policeman came walking by, but the king's sons were stymied. Knowing that in order to examine the officer's head they must first dislodge his helmet, they ran out of ideas as to how they could achieve their objective. They had never done that sort of thing before.

By the most fortuitous set of coincidences, there happened to be a scruffy little cockney kid standing near who had developed considerable skill in dislodging policemen's helmets with a small stone and unerring aim. He was offered a shilling if he would do the dirty work for the princes, and with a dexterous flick of the wrist, the stone flew to its target, the helmet fell to the ground, and a bald head was revealed in all its glory.

"You owe me a shilling," said the delighted winner, even though they had not proved that all fat policeman had bald heads—just one! But they knew nothing of statistical analysis, so his claim went unchallenged. They were busy settling debts and winnings and completely forgot about the offended officer, who descended upon them loudly protesting "the attack on his person during the course of his duty as he was proceeding in a westerly direction."

"What's your name?" he demanded of the taller boy.

"I'm the Prince of Wales," the boy replied.

"What? I never heard such impudence. Give me your name."

"I am the Prince of Wales," he insisted.

"I don't believe you, but I'll write it down," the officer grunted.

"And what's your name?' the policeman asked, turning to the younger prince.

"I am the Duke of Kent," he answered, "and this is my brother, the Prince of Wales."

"I don't believe you either." He snorted in disgust, and then turning to the scruffy little kid from the east end of London, he asked, "And who are you?"

The boy nudged his two new friends and partners in crime and said, "Don't worry, boys. I won't let you down." Then drawing himself up to his full height he declared, "Officer, I'm the Archbishop of Canterbury!"

History does not record how this intriguing saga ended, but curiosity wants to know why no one believed the prince's story. The answer—and the moral of the story—is not hard to find. Nobody believes a boy is a king's son if he behaves like a young thug. Like everybody else, young princes need to watch their step and walk the talk if they want to be taken seriously.

> Those who have experienced the kingdom desire earnestly to express the kingdom.

With this in mind, those who have *experienced* the kingdom—have been born again—desire earnestly to *express* the kingdom—that is, live out the righteousness of the kingdom. This becomes their top priority.

The next question then is: How do you do that?

Paul the apostle gave us a clearly defined starting point

when he wrote to the Corinthians, "The kingdom of God is not a matter of talk but of power" (1 Corinthians 4:20). He said this because he was tired of the excess verbiage coming from his detractors. He was in effect challenging them to stop the talk and walk the walk. And a powerfully convincing walk was what he had in mind. It's not a matter of talk—it's a matter of *power*. But what kind of power expresses the kingdom? It's the Spirit-driven power of a transformed life. That is what Paul wanted to see—and that is what Jesus said should be the top priority. Remember? First the kingdom of God and His righteousness.

When I was a Cub Scout in England, with fingers to my cap I promised in a squeaky voice that I would try to do "a good turn" to somebody every day. That became a priority for me for about a week, if I remember rightly. The idea was resurrected in my mind recently when I heard a preacher admonishing his congregation to "do an outrageous act of kindness to someone every day." Both of these sentiments are noble and good as far as interpersonal relationships are concerned, but thinking in terms of a lifestyle focused on expressing the power of a Spirit-transformed life—the righteousness of the kingdom—is closer to what Jesus taught.

On another occasion Paul wrote to the Roman believers. They were apparently getting into a strong debate—or disagreement—over what kind of food and drink believers should partake of. Obviously the issue was generating strong feelings. Paul did not summarily dismiss their concerns, but put them in perspective: "The kingdom of God is not a matter of eating and drinking, but of righteousness, peace and joy in the Holy Spirit, because anyone who serves Christ in this way is pleasing to God and approved by men" (Romans 14:17–18).

Note that *righteousness* appears again, coupled this time with *joy* and *peace*. Quality of life is what matters—kingdom behavior is what counts. Why? Because this kind of living pleases God and meets with human approval too. That just about covers everything, doesn't it? But we can take this a step further. Paul developed the idea of righteous living when he told the Ephesian Christians, "Live as children of light (for the fruit of light consists in all goodness, righteousness and truth) and find out what pleases the Lord" (Ephesians 5:8–10).

Now look carefully at the cluster of fruit gathered around righteousness—joy, peace, goodness, and truth.

Joy is more than being happy. Lots of people have made it their goal to be happy, but because often their happiness is related to their happenings, which they cannot control, they spend a lot of unhappy time because of unwanted happenings. Joy is a deep-rooted sense of well-being even when things happen to happen...the way we don't want them to happen.

Then there is "peace." Most people would love to have a peaceful life. Some will even settle for "peace at any price." In their minds peace comes from the eradication of stress or after the cessation of hostilities. But as stress will never be eliminated and wars will never cease, we probably should say good-bye to that kind of peace. The peace of which the Bible speaks has little or nothing to do with stress or hostilities, but everything to do with order. The deep-rooted sense that whatever my external circumstances, I know deep in my heart that things are in order between my God and me.

> The peace of which the Bible speaks has everything to do with order.

You will note that I have just used the phrase *deep-rooted sense* on two occasions. For a good reason. Because joy and peace well up within the lives of those who, having been born again through the action of the Holy Spirit, now order their lives in the power of the Holy Spirit to do what is right before God.

And what does this have to do with putting first things first and deterring the time bandits that prowl? Everything. Because now the overriding goal of my life is to do what is right in God's eyes, knowing it will please Him, knowing it will meet with wide approval, and knowing full well that the result will be inner peace and joy. You can't beat an assurance like that!

And neither can the bandits.

Chapter Nine

NOW FOR THE CHALLENGE

At this point I feel compelled to share with you one or two little personal secrets. Nothing earth shattering. Here they are. I like to feel comfortable. I like to be popular and I prefer activities that prove profitable. But I think you will understand because they seem to be quite common preferences. Comfortable, popular, and profitable.

For example, I have spent far too much of my life on airplanes. Far too often I have been placed in the center seat between two large people. Their excess poundage has lapped over into my territory on the right and the left. With knees wedged under the seat in front and the tray table pressing relentlessly in my abdominal cavity, my discomfort is assured when the passenger in front reclines his seat so that his headrest abuts my nose. The joys of air travel defy description—they have to be experienced to be appreciated.

But I have good news. Having served my time in such invidious circumstances, I have amassed hundreds of thousands of air miles. Rightly traded, these air miles now allow me to ascend to Business Class, where people are treated as people and airlines recognize that having to sit with your feet in your pockets for eight hours is not conducive to producing happy, well-rested travelers. All that to say, I like my comfort!

I also much prefer to be popular than the target of abuse and hatred. Years ago I played in a Rugby match featuring the Royal Marine Commandos versus the Devon County Police. Pre-match discussions made it clear that the majority of my team—the Marines—had at some time or other been on the wrong end of the professional services of members of the other team—the Police. Scores were going to be settled on the field of play. (That's right, they called it the field of *play!*)

Unfortunately, during the game I collided heavily with one of the police team's players, and he came off second best with fractured ribs. His colleagues were convinced that I had injured him intentionally and gathered round me in most menacing fashion, shouting, gesticulating, and screaming for revenge. But my Commando friends surrounded me, took me to relative safety so that I survived the balance of the game, and I have so far lived happily ever after. I must admit that I prefer to be popular rather than reviled.

Then there is the matter of profitability. When I was a young bank clerk, I noticed that one of our customers seemed to have an uncanny feel for the stock market. He knew how to buy low and sell high. He never missed. So one day when he bought some stock, I for the first time in my life did the same thing. Almost immediately the stock soared, and with it went my spirits. Shortly after buying the stock he sold his, but for some reason I kept mine. Each day I rushed to the financial paper to check on my investment. When it went up so did I, when it came down I did too. I learned something about myself—I had a distinct interest in making a profit and a deep distaste for losing.

> Daily living gives me continual opportunities to reevaluate my priorities.

So there you have it—an insight into Stuart Briscoe. He's a normal sort of guy who likes what is comfortable, popular, and profitable. So what's so strange about that?

Nothing! Nothing at all.

But as Shakespeare would say, here's "the rub." What does it mean to make the kingdom a priority? To be committed to "goodness, righteousness, and truth."

"Ah yes," you say, "My goal is to enjoy what is comfortable, popular, and profitable *in the context of* goodness, righteousness, and truth."

Great. But don't forget the rub.

- What happens if that which is good is not comfortable?
- And what do we do if what is right is not profitable?
- And how do we handle situations where the truth is not popular?

Now, I assure you that I am not posing hypothetical issues here. These are the sort of things I bump into in the normal course of events, and given my natural propensities to comfort, popularity, and profitability, they present regular challenges to me. That's the bad news! The good news, of course, is that daily living gives me continual opportunities to reevaluate my priorities.

For example, around the same time as I was following the fortunes of the aforementioned client at the bank where I worked, I was told by the manager one day, "If Mrs. Jones calls, tell her I'm out of the office."

As we were the only two men in the small branch, I was

surprised to hear that he was leaving me alone. So I replied, "Oh! Are you going out?"

He was not known for patience and replied sharply, "Of course I'm not going out! Just tell her I'm out."

"But," I replied hastily, " I can't say you're out if you're in."

He replied, " If you know what's good for you, you can certainly do what you're told."

I was very young and very scared and totally confused. This was new, and I did not like what I was hearing. This man who during my relatively short business career had been very good to me, greatly encouraging and assisting me in my promotions, had suddenly shown a side I had never seen before.

In a very shaky voice I said, "I'm sorry. I can't do that." He lost his temper completely, threw papers in the air, and shouted, "You will do what you're told!"

"I am so sorry I have offended you," I said. "But I don't know why you're angry with me. All I have done is tell you that I will not tell a lie for you. Why are you angry? You should be glad in the knowledge that if I won't tell a lie for you, I won't tell a lie *to* you. You can trust me."

Making the kingdom a priority involves choosing truth over popularity.

He stormed out of the room. But give him credit, he

returned about an hour later and said, "I am so sorry. And you need to know one thing. I will see that you go to the top of this bank. We need people of integrity."

Now that's what I mean by making the kingdom a priority. It involves choosing truth over popularity when the two are in conflict. I was fortunate. Choosing truth over popularity can cost you.

There's the sort of thing that my friend Ray encountered. He was a new believer. Shortly after coming to faith—or being born again—he asked me if he could meet with me once a week. I gladly agreed, and as I had just bought a new book on Christian theology, I suggested we read one hundred pages each week and meet to discuss what we had read. He happily agreed. But I soon regretted making such a heavy demand on a new believer. I couldn't keep up with him! He quickly became as knowledgeable as he was committed. But he surprised me one day by telling me that he was quitting his job. I knew he enjoyed his work and was capable and successful at his profession, so I wondered why he was quitting.

"Because," he said, "we've been talking about a believer's lifestyle being important, and mine is not consistent."

"In what way?" I asked, surprised.

"In my profession it is impossible to make a living and be honest. I am committed to honesty, so the job has to go." In other words, when it came down to a choice between what is profitable and what is right, he decided for what is right. He had his priorities focused on the kingdom. (Incidentally, I knew people in his line of business who were both honest and successful, and he went to work for them.)

It doesn't get any easier when we consider the conflict that can arise between doing what is good and being comfortable. Quite a long time ago I preached a sermon in which I spoke out against abortion on demand. There was a lot of positive response to what I said, and it was obvious that the church as a whole strongly agreed with my position. But one of my young associate pastors talked to me afterward and said, "You know, Stuart, you told us all what you're against, but didn't say a word about what you're for."

"What do you mean?" I inquired.

"Well my guess is that there were probably some young women in the congregation today who are pregnant, feeling guilty, and frightened with nowhere to turn. And you made them feel more guilty."

"Don't you agree with what I said about abortion?" I asked him.

"You know I do. But what are we doing to help those who are considering abortion because they think they have no alternative? What kind of alternatives are we as a church offering?"

"You're right!" I said to him. "And you're fired!" He

knew he wasn't, and we laughed and put our heads together to see what we could do as a church. (He's still on staff, by the way.)

The next week, I proposed to the congregation that we needed families who would volunteer to take in to their homes young women who were pregnant out of wedlock with a view to assisting them during their pregnancy and helping them with their babies. I noticed something very interesting. While there had been strong approval for my talk the previous week when I outlined the evils of abortion on demand, there was a remarkable lack of response to the suggestion that families take in some of the young women in question.

Why?

I hesitate to say. There are probably numerous reasons. But I suspect one of them might be that while everybody would agree that taking a needy girl into a loving, caring family for a brief time would be good, it would also disrupt family life and therefore be uncomfortable.

There's the rub again.

I have no quarrel with those who want to be comfortable, popular, and profitable—after all, I am one of them.

I need to face up to my selfishness and see life through kingdom eyes.

But I need to face up to my selfishness and see life through kingdom eyes. And when I do, my priorities change to a focus on goodness, righteousness, and truth. Yours will too.

Chapter Ten

KINGDOM
EXPANSION

When you get to my age—seventy-three—your body starts to work like an old car. So you take it in for repairs and tune-ups. That's what I did this week. First I went to see my ophthalmologist. He's a fine man in his early forties. Tall, good looking, successful, lovely wife, great kids. After the usual examination and drops in the eyes, he concluded that I did not need a white cane or a guide dog and pronounced me fit to carry on.

Then he pushed back his chair and said, "You know, I've been on two or three trips to the Philippines. I love it. We go to the villages and I take stacks of lenses and frames—new ones—and I give examinations and fit the people up. And we share the gospel with them—I just love it. But now with the terror alerts in the region of the Philippines, we haven't been able to return. I miss it so much. In fact, I would really like to work gradually to an early retirement, giving more of my time to that kind of work until I could give all my time to working in places where the people have nothing. But in the meantime, do you have anywhere I could go on maybe two or three trips a year?"

I looked at this young man busy fulfilling the American dream and noticed the intensity with which he spoke, the passion in his voice, and I knew he'd been working on his priorities. By the way, I had lots of ideas for him!

> Jesus reminded the disciples that their task was to take the kingdom to all people.

Later in the week I visited the dentist. After the usual scraping and chipping by the hygienist, I was examined by my friend the dentist and apart from one minor task was once again pronounced fit to carry on. Then the dentist pushed back his chair and said, "You know, Stuart, I've been thinking. There's an orphanage out in Armenia, and they have such needs there and I've been asked to go and help them. I'd love to do it, but there are so many places and so many needs and I'm so busy teaching and leading in my church here that I don't know whether I should go or not."

I noted the seriousness in his voice, the earnestness with which he was looking at his life in the context of a needy world, and I knew he'd been checking his priorities.

You see, when the kingdom is first, the extension of that kingdom becomes a matter of major interest and concern. But why? Simply because Jesus made it clear right from the beginning of His ministry that He had come to proclaim the Good News of the kingdom, and at the end of His ministry on earth, He reminded His little group of disciples that their task was to take the kingdom to all people.

In fact, I find it very interesting that after Jesus rose again He did not return immediately to heaven. I'm sure He would have liked that very much. But for forty days He stayed around, regularly visiting the disciples and talking to them about—you guessed it—*the kingdom*. Apparently He delayed His return to make sure they understood the seriousness of their calling. They had to get news of the kingdom out to the whole world. As He told them this and reemphasized it for their benefit, I suspect they remembered His solemn and startling words just a few days earlier when, having talked to them about future events, He said, "This gospel of the kingdom will be preached in the whole world, as a testimony to all nations, and then the end will come" (Matthew 24:14).

So in addition to *experiencing* and *expressing* the kingdom as a priority we now must add *extending* the kingdom. That is what was making such an impression on the minds and lifestyles of my ophthalmologist and my dentist.

Neither of these men was claiming a spectacular vision or an emotional call. They were not planning to pack up their businesses and their families and board a banana boat for Bongo. They were looking realistically at their obligations and skills, their aspirations and priorities, and concluding that they as professional men should be actively involved in expanding the kingdom. They were already doing it at home in their daily lives, but the priority of extending the kingdom was pushing them into a reevaluation of the way they were utilizing their skills and distributing their resources.

In my case it was different. As a young man in my twenties, I had become active in reaching out to the thousands of British young people who were completely unchurched. My friends and I had discovered a way to reach them, and as a result I was spending most of my spare time working in dark and dingy dives where the kids congregated to listen to their music, grow their hair, and drink coffee—and listen to the gospel of the kingdom if it was presented in language they understood in a manner to which they could relate. My concern to see the extension of the kingdom into the lives of these young people became so overpowering that it took total precedence over my banking career, so that in my case it called for a resignation from the business world and a positive response to a call to youth ministry.

Whether the recognition of a believer's privilege and responsibility to be involved in the kingdom's expansion as a matter of priority leads to a reorientation of resources and a reevaluation of skills (as in the case of the dentist and the ophthalmologist) or a complete career change (as in my case) is only a matter of degree. The issue is, if I embrace "first the kingdom" as my principle of operation, then that means among other things a commitment to extending the kingdom in my area of influence.

Now, I think I can hear murmuring in the distance. I think you are saying—under your breath—*Where does he think I'm going to find the time to add "extending the kingdom" on to everything else?*

I knew it! But I'm not advocating additions to your DayTimer; I'm encouraging revisions to your way of thinking. Like at the beginning of the day saying, *All right, Lord, here we go again. Today I have this, that, and the other to do, and I don't need anything else added to my schedule. So would You please help me to go through today thinking* kingdom? *So that in the contacts I make and the decisions at which I arrive, and the responses I give I will concentrate on expressing and extending Your kingdom rather than instinctively thinking about my little empire.*

Try it. This may sound difficult and you may be inclined to think it impractical. But I assure you that fresh mind-sets can be developed and old habits can be changed. For the better!

Chapter Eleven

WHAT ABOUT
WORRY?

A mother and her young son were out walking in the woods one fine day. She had recently been influenced by teaching that suggested that minds can triumph over matter. Suddenly they encountered a bear. The young boy turned to run, but his mother stopped him. "There's nothing to be frightened of," she told him. "The bear can't hurt us. You know that and I know that."

"I know you know that and I know I know that," said the terrified youngster, "but does the bear know that?"

It's all right for teachers to propound theories, but once the students get out of the classroom, where they meet the action, the theories imbibed need to be applied. Before the bear showed up, the boy apparently had no doubts that his mother had grasped a powerful theory. But the appearance of a few hundred pounds of hungry carnivore gave him pause for thought. And the doubts were not going to go away while the bear stood before him licking his chops.

So it is with biblical teaching. Take the teaching about not worrying. Jesus did say that we shouldn't worry about many of the things that we do worry about. In a church service where all is serene and the preacher is convincing, it really is amazing how rapidly worries dissipate. And how amazing is the speed with which they recover and return! Unless of course we have taken to heart the whole teaching. It's when we make the kingdom the top priority that we're in a position to cope with the normal worries of life. And the reason? Because Jesus was saying, in effect, "If you look after the things that concern Me, I will care for the things that worry you."

When James Hudson Taylor III, the grandson of the famous missionary, was a young boy, he and his siblings were sent off to boarding school in Malaya while their par-

> When we make the kingdom the top priority, we're in a position to cope with the normal worries of life.

ents continued their missionary work in a remote area of China. World War II broke out, and young James, his siblings, and hundreds of other students were captured by the Japanese forces and placed in an internment camp. For a number of years, parents and children had no contact with each other. Naturally Mr. and Mrs. Taylor were deeply perturbed about their children, but when the family was finally reunited unharmed, Mrs. Taylor recounted how she was convinced that the Lord had conveyed to her a simple but profound message: "You look after the things that matter to Me, and I will look after the ones who matter to you." And on the strength of this conviction she had been able to carry on.

Hopefully none of us will ever be put in such a position, but we will no doubt encounter testing times when worry takes over and the kingdom slips from first place in our priorities.

Perhaps we need to make a more definite connection between kingdom priorities and victory over worry. What is the connection? How does it work? It's all about the King—King Jesus—who reigns triumphant on the throne of heaven, biding His time until the right moment, when He returns to defeat His enemies, destroy evil, establish His eternal kingdom, and create a new heaven and new earth. It is King Jesus who triumphed over death by His glorious resurrection and who lives in the power of an endless life.

King Jesus, who in the person of the Holy Spirit has taken up residence in the hearts and lives of believers in order that He might strengthen them with might in their innermost beings. It is He who takes charge of the lives of His followers and who commits Himself to their well-being.

Paul told the Philippian believers:

> Do not be anxious about anything, but in everything by prayer and petition with thanksgiving present your requests to God. And the peace of God, which transcends all understanding, will guard your hearts and your minds in Christ Jesus.
>
> PHILIPPIANS 4:6–7

So what do we have to do? We have to pray! How? With petitions and thanksgiving. Praying is the talking part of the relationship we have with the Lord. The listening part is when we take time to immerse ourselves in His Word, the Bible. Like all good relationships, communication is vital. And communication involves listening and talking. So healthy believing always includes effective praying.

How should we pray? We could start with something like this:

> *Lord, I'm a worrier. You know it, I know it, and I also know that I should not be spending my time wor-*

rying about things. But they are important to me.
That's the problem—they are too important to me.
The kingdom should be most important, but these
other things take precedence all too easily. I need Your
help in really believing that if I put the kingdom first,
You, the King, will make my concerns a matter of pri-
ority for You.

I ask that Your Spirit will work in my heart, con-
vincing me that if I put my energies into experienc-
ing, expressing, and enlarging the kingdom, You will
exert divine power on my behalf in the mundane
matters that I think only I can handle. I do not want
to act irresponsibly by trusting You to do what You
told me to do, but I also do not want to be unbeliev-
ing either. Lord, I believe. Please help my unbelief.

Then you can bring your petitions about certain areas
of worry to Him, knowing that you have His attention and
His concern. List them, tell Him, be frank, be straightforward. Ask Him to do for you what in principle He has said
He will do for all His children.

But you must do it with thanksgiving. Why? Because
approaching the throne of God is such a privilege that we
should never cease to thank Him for it. Secondly, "thank
you" is the language of faith. Saying thank you is not only
a matter of courteous acknowledgment of audience with

the King, but it also indicates that you believe you have been heard and that the answers that are best for you are on their way.

Then expect the promised peace that transcends understanding to filter into your life. That does not mean everything will come up roses. Peace in idyllic circumstances is easily understood. Prioritizing the kingdom may mean less than ideal circumstances, challenges, and costs to be paid, but it also means a release from chronic worry and an experience of a deep-rooted knowledge that all is well.

Peace in such circumstances is truly beyond understanding.

Chapter Twelve

ALL THESE THINGS...

Did you hear about the man who slept with his head in the refrigerator and his feet in the oven? He wanted to keep both extremes in balance. I suppose he estimated that he was avoiding extremes and maintaining an average body temperature. But his position was certainly precarious and uncomfortable!

That's how it is with extremes. For example, you can become so spiritually minded that you are of no earthly use. Or your thinking can be so earthbound that it lacks spiritual content and vision. This is certainly the case when we discuss priorities. The practically minded person may have techniques and systems by which he governs his life. No one tried harder to work on this basis than Benjamin Franklin. He listed thirteen "cardinal virtues," concentrated on each of them for a week, and calculated that he could do this four times every year. But disciplined as he was, he quit before completing the first thirteen-week cycle, saying that perfection was not such a worthy goal after all and that "a benevolent man should allow a few faults in himself, to keep his friends in countenance." A superb piece of rationalization. In Franklin's case, the spiritual dimension was missing.

Jesus did not dismiss the practical issues.

On the other hand, you may be thinking that my emphasis on the kingdom as the number one priority is too spiritual and not practical enough. Jesus did not dismiss the practical issues, as we have already seen. He said three things about them: first, that they were not all-important; second, that they were not unimportant; third that if the kingdom was the top priority, they would be put in their proper place and cared for appropriately. His exact words, you may remember, were:

> "Seek first his kingdom and his righteousness, and all these things will be given to you as well."
>
> MATTHEW 6:33

The "things" He said would be *given* to them—suggesting that if they accepted the kingdom as their business, He would assume responsibility for those "things"—were what they were anxious about, active in, and ambitious for. I identified them earlier as:

- food
- fashion
- fitness
- future
- finances

They are all eminently practical issues, and the spiritually practical person—or, if you prefer, the practically spiritual person—understands how they fit into the lifestyle of the one who has made the kingdom his top priority. But how does it work?

Let's take them one at a time.

Food

As I write, the airwaves are full of food news. Cookery books top the bestseller lists, followed closely—and ironically—by diet books. The latter apparently being the antidote to the former. The Atkins diet has made a roaring comeback, and bread companies are running scared. They are advertising how few carbs their breads contain while mad cow disease has McDonald's and Outback Steakhouse alarmed. Why all this emphasis on food? Because food is big. So are the people overindulging in it. So big in fact that the government is getting in the act and instituting another war—this time the war on obesity.

While all this is going on in the affluent West, twenty-three children die from malnutrition every minute in other parts of the world. The *Economist* magazine points out that formerly the rich were obese and the poor were thin, but now in the West the rich are thin and the poor are obese because they are not eating wisely and their nutritional intake is unbalanced.

What should I do about all this? I should approach my eating as a kingdom person, which means first of all I do not indulge myself—we used to call it gluttony—because gluttony is a sin and I'm seeking to display righteousness. Second, because I have a concern for the spread of the king-dom message and I know that it falls on deaf ears if the people are dead, I budget my resources, particularly those spent on luxury food, so that I can in some measure allevi-ate the sufferings of the unfortunate. You can think of other ways.

FASHION

In the West the fashion issue for men appears to be whether they should "dress for success," which can easily lead to excess, or whether they should emulate the "Busters" and

"Gen X-ers" and "Gen Y-ers"—and I know not what other generations—and "dress down," which appears to mean declaring war on jackets and neckties. The two approaches while heading in opposite directions are both amazingly self-conscious and driven by self-expression.

Women, on the other hand, dress with great care, taking into account weather, latest style, who they are meeting, where they are meeting them, what they are hoping to achieve, what they wore at the last meeting, and a host of other things that I as a mere male have never understood.

But I do understand what happened to me in the early days of my pastoral ministry. The church where I ministered was a relatively conservative suburban fellowship—until we had a wonderful influx of about one hundred refugees from the Jesus Movement. The regulars dressed up for church in their "Sunday best"; our newfound brothers and sisters dressed in Goodwill chic. One day a young man, hirsute and earnest, came to me and said, "Stuart, I think you're sincere, but I can't believe what you're saying because you must have paid a hundred dollars for that suit, and Jesus never would have wasted that much money on clothes. So I'm not going to listen to you anymore."

"It's funny you should say that," I replied, "because earlier this week the chairman of the board told me to wear more expensive clothes because the way I dress, people would think the church wasn't paying me enough!"

That was when I realized that for the sake of the kingdom I needed to think a little more clearly about the fashion statement I was making without being aware that I was making one! It was affecting my kingdom effectiveness.

So instead of just wearing what I wanted to wear and doing what I wanted to do, I began to think about the image I was projecting. On occasion, some sloppy comfortable clothes were discarded for the sake of the kingdom where they would have seemed inappropriate to the people with whom I wished to communicate. Other times my preferred style of clothes, which made me look like a dinosaur to the ones to whom I was ministering, were retired prematurely. Personal preferences no longer dominated. Bigger issues prevailed.

FITNESS

I told you earlier about the football coaches who descended upon me years ago and reminded me that when my physical body quit, my spiritual ministry would end and so I needed to concentrate on my physical fitness. Apart from the problem of time constraints, I also had to deal with issues of motivation. Particularly in the middle of a Wisconsin winter! Early mornings in zero temperatures on icy roads were not my idea of paradise. Seeing my weight drop because of running, feeling the exhilaration of icicles melting off my beard in the shower, or even the satisfaction of seeing my time improve could not always keep me going.

But the thought of the kingdom could, because the words of my friends, the coaches, rang in my ears. For the sake of the kingdom, I could not in good conscience become a couch potato, overweight and lazy, when the kingdom needed people slimmed down for action and toned up for the struggle. And I had no doubt that physical fitness could make a difference in my ability to be a kingdom person.

> For the sake of the kingdom, I could not in good conscience become a couch potato.

FUTURE

The people Jesus was dealing with were worrying about adding time to their lifespan, and He made it clear to them that their worrying would not help. If He'd wished to fast-forward and explain modern science to them, He could have shown that worry is counterproductive when it comes to longevity.

In the modern Western world, the search for the secret of eternal youth goes on apace. Grey hairs are tinted, wrinkles are tucked, and retirement villages are well stocked with play-grounds and "fun things to do." It seems as if the thought of aging and gradually completing a full life must be shunned and the "evil day" postponed ad infinitum. Financial security that will allow for a long and full retirement becomes a goal early in life for many.

But kingdom people see things differently. They believe they have only one life to live, and that life should be devoted primarily to experiencing, expressing, and expanding the kingdom. Accordingly they look at the future as a precious gift from the King granted to them in order that they might fulfill a divinely granted role in a world that either operates on the basis of the "present evil age" or "the kingdom of our God."

Kingdom people view each new day as the first day of the rest of their lives and look for ways to be channels of blessing and agents of change in it. They leave the details of their engagement with the world in which the King has chosen to leave them up to Him.

FINANCES

"Laying up treasures on earth" is a very popular objective in our world. And it is not hard to figure out why this should be. Treasures on earth can make life more pleasant, much easier, and sometimes even longer. People of means live in bigger houses, stay in nicer places, drive faster cars, fly in better seats, hire people to do what they don't want to do, and generally do very well for themselves. So who wouldn't make laying up treasures on earth a priority?

Kingdom people! They have listened to Jesus, who warned against being so wrapped up with the amassing of wealth for immediate gratification and future security that the larger issues of why we are here and where we are going when we're through down here become blurred.

> Jesus warned against being wrapped up with the amassing of wealth.

Greed does not express the kingdom; self-absorption does not promote the King; hoarding does not extend the kingdom.

We should work hard because humans were designed to work. We should produce materials or services of value to our fellow men, and we should accept our share of the value as a legitimate remuneration for effort expended. But we should remember always that it is God who gives the power to get wealth. How's that? Because He gives us the energy, the time, and the skills, which when expended in meaningful labor produce value. Kingdom people look at the value received as a reward for effort expended, for skills utilized, for time well spent, but they never forget that all these value-producing factors were gifts in the first place. And they look at the products as gifts too—gifts to be administered as stewards, as kingdom people, and utilized in a thousand ways to express and expand the kingdom.

It is significant that Jesus did not condemn people for being concerned and interested in food, fashion, fitness, and other assorted items beginning with *f.* In fact, He showed that He was interested and concerned about them too. But His concern was that they should be put in proper perspective. He demonstrated this when He assured His listeners that when the kingdom was in the right place, everything else would be there too. They would sort out their thinking, desiring, and acting about all these life issues, and life would be richer, fuller, and more significant because it would honor the King and promote the kingdom.

REDEEMING THE TIME

My younger son, when he was a teenager, once told the chairman of a meeting who had introduced me that I didn't really need an introduction, but that I desperately needed a conclusion. I have no doubt you agree. So here it is!

1. Be honest! Do you feel that your life is out of control? That there aren't enough hours in the day? And that you spend too much time stressed and frustrated?
2. Are you ready to admit that your existing priorities should be carefully examined?
3. Do you accept the principle that the kingdom of God should take precedence over everything else?

4. Have you ever consciously yielded your past, present, and future to the Lord Jesus, asking Him to forgive your past, control your present, and secure your future?

5. Are you willing to embrace each day as twenty-four hours full of opportunities to experience and express and extend the kingdom in your thought patterns, your decisions, and your actions?

6. Do you really believe that the King who calls you to this lifestyle will empower you by His Spirit to live it out?

7. Are you excited about seeing off those time bandits and welcoming the King who gave you the gift of life, filled it with hours and minutes, and showed you how to fill them full?

First things first—first the kingdom!

JILL BRISCOE

What if He's asking you to pour out more than you can give? Step into the forward motion of God's love—and find the power of the Holy Spirit!

A Little Pot of Oil
A Life Overflowing